Solution-Focused Living
TRUST THE PROCESS
THROUGH AFFIRMATIONS

Interior photographs taken by the author and used with permission.

Nancy Moorhouse
Choteau, Montana

Limits of Liability
The author and publisher shall not be liable for your misuse of this material. This book is strictly for informational and educational purposes.

Disclaimer
This book educates and entertain. The author and/or publisher guarantee no one following these techniques, suggestions, tips, ideas, or strategies will become successful. The author and/or publisher shall have neither liability nor responsibility to anyone regarding any loss or damage caused, or alleged to be caused, directly or indirectly by the information in this book.

Paperback: 979-8-9925484-9-5
eBook: 979-8-9925484-8-8

Solution-Focused Living

TRUST THE PROCESS
THROUGH AFFIRMATIONS

BY NANCY MOORHOUSE

CONTACT ME

Scoop, Crush & Rocks: Making Profit, Playing Nice: Life Lessons from the Gravel Pit, is available for purchase from Amazon:

https://www.amazon.com/dp/B0776MXZG1/
or on
www.nancymoorhouse.com.

I would enjoy reading how these affirmations have helped and inspired you! If you like, leave me an email at scoopcrush@gmail.com.

DEDICATION

For Elijah

OTHER WRITINGS

Through the school of hard knocks, Nancy Moorhouse spent her first career creating from scratch, a safe production culture for a family-owned construction and aggregate company. Her first book, *Scoop, Crush & Rocks: Making Profit, Playing Nice: Life Lessons from the Gravel Pit*, was about a manager's journey working in the rock business.

Nancy's other writings can be found in the 2014 and 2023 *Celebrating 365 Days of Gratitude* books. Her industry focused publications can be found on the Insurance Thought Leadership website. Her next work is based on her dad's World War II letters written home from 1944 – 1946.

INTRODUCTION

Life is full of twists and turns, sometimes a school of hard knocks with unexpected detours. There are valleys of despair and mountaintops of triumph. Every step we take shapes who we are. Some steps are steady; others falter. For me, many steps have been uphill climbs through tough trials, awkward moments, frustration, failures and tears. Each challenge, though, has taught me to trust the process. Bigger and better lies ahead.

I worked my first career in the construction and aggregates industry. Building a safe production culture from scratch showed me the value of dedicated front-line workers wanting to do the best job they could within the defined management systems and processes. The culture change didn't come about by chance, it came from clear actions, steady effort, and faith in the outcome.

Basic leadership principles of beginning with the end in mind, listening to those who had answers and integrating subtle process changes made for enhanced, profit-retention processes for the company. Life works the same way. Each moment, even the hard ones, is part of a bigger plan. These moments guide us toward personal and spiritual growth.

My first book, *Scoop, Crush & Rocks: Making Profit, Playing Nice*, was about the life lessons learned from the gravel pit. This book you have in your hands is different. It's about affirmations and the mindset shifts which continue to help me through life's ups and downs.

Life's circle reminds us that everything is connected. Challenges repeat themselves until we learn their lessons. This book, *Solution-Focused Living: Trust the Process Through Affirmations*, reflects that truth. It invites you to see challenges as opportunities. Each setback is a step forward on the journey to fulfillment.

Affirmations aren't quick fixes. They help you see things differently, refocus, and stay strong. They're about believing in yourself and the path you're on.

May this book become your companion. Let it encourage you and remind you to trust the process—even when the road ahead looks uncertain. May these pages bring you hope, strength and perseverance to carry on.

Nancy

STARTING
WHERE YOU ARE

"You can't go back and change the beginning, but you can start where you are and change the ending."
C.S. Lewis (1898-1963)

Every journey begins in the present moment. Where you are right now may feel messy, uncertain, or overwhelming. Even so, it is the perfect place to start. Accepting your current reality is the first step toward creating the future you want. This section focuses on embracing who you are today. Small actions, taken one step at a time, can lead to meaningful change. By staying grounded in the present, you create opportunities for progress and growth.

I accept where I
am in this moment,
knowing it is the
perfect place to begin.

I trust that every step I take, no matter how small, brings me closer to my goals.

I release any judgment
about my current
situation and embrace it
as part of my journey.

I am capable of growth
and change, starting
right here, right now.

I honor the lessons of today as they guide me toward a brighter tomorrow.

I choose to focus on
progress, not perfection,
as I move forward.

I welcome the opportunities that come with being present and aware in this moment.

I have everything I need within me to take the first step toward positive change.

EMBRACING
CHANGE

"Win as if you were used to it,
lose as if you enjoyed it for a change."
Ralph Waldo Emerson (1803 - 1882)

Change is a part of life. It can feel uncomfortable or even scary. But change is also where growth happens. By letting go of what no longer serves you, you create space for new possibilities. This section is about welcoming change with an open heart. Each step forward brings you closer to the life you want.

I welcome change
as an opportunity to
grow and learn.

I trust myself to adapt and thrive in any situation.

I let go of fear and
embrace the possibilities
that change brings.

I release what no longer
serves me to make
room for the new.

I am resilient and capable of navigating life's transitions.

I see change as a chance
to create a better
version of myself.

I remain open to the
lessons and blessings
that come with change.

I choose to move
forward with courage
and confidence.

OVERCOMING
OBSTACLES

"With everything that has happened to you, you can either feel sorry for yourself or treat what has happened as a gift. Everything is either an opportunity to grow or an obstacle to keep you from growing. You get to choose!"
Wayne Dyer (1940 – 2015)

Obstacles are a natural part of any journey. They test your strength and teach you valuable lessons. Facing challenges can feel difficult, but each is an opportunity to grow stronger. This section is about finding courage in tough moments. With the right mindset, every obstacle can become a stepping stone toward success.

I face challenges
with strength and
determination.

Every obstacle I encounter is an opportunity to grow.

I trust my ability to
find solutions and
move forward.

I am resilient and
capable of overcoming
anything in my path.

I learn from difficulties
and use them to
become stronger.

I stay focused on my process, my goals, no matter the challenges I face.

I believe in my power
to turn setbacks
into comebacks.

I approach obstacles
with courage and a
positive mindset.

CULTIVATING
PATIENCE

*"Knowing trees, I understand the meaning
of patience. Knowing grass, I can
appreciate persistence."
Hal Borland (1900-1978)
writer, journalist and naturalist.*

Patience is an essential part of trusting the process. It reminds us that growth takes time and progress doesn't happen overnight. While waiting can feel challenging, it allows us to build resilience and faith in the journey. This section is about embracing the pauses and trusting that each moment is leading you toward your goals. With patience, you create space for the process to unfold as it's meant to.

I trust the process and
allow things to unfold
in their own time.

I embrace moments of waiting as opportunities for growth.

I remain calm and
steady, knowing progress
is being made.

I release the need to rush and trust that everything happens at the right time.

I find peace in the
pauses and strength
in the stillness.

I am patient with myself and my journey, knowing each step has value.

I trust that delays are not denials but redirections toward something better.

I welcome each day
with faith I am moving
closer to my goals.

BUILDING
CONFIDENCE

*"You build on failure. You use it as a
stepping stone. Close the door on the past.
You don't try to forget the mistakes, but you
don't dwell on it. You don't let it have any of
your energy, or any of your time,
or any of your space."*
Singer/songwriter Johnny Cash
(1932 – 2003)

Through failures, we can build confidence. Confidence is built one step at a time. It comes from trusting yourself and recognizing your strengths. Believing in your abilities helps you face challenges with courage. This section is about developing the self-assurance to move forward. When you trust yourself, you can achieve anything within your control.

I trust myself and
my ability to handle
whatever comes my way.

I believe in my strengths
and use them to
achieve my goals.

I am capable, worthy,
and deserving of success.

I face challenges
with courage and
self-assurance.

I let go of doubt and embrace my inner power.

I learn and grow with every experience, building my confidence each day.

I am proud of who I
am and the progress
I've made.

I trust my decisions
and stand strong
in my choices.

FINDING
GRATITUDE

"Life with God is not immunity from difficulties, but peace in difficulties."
C.S. Lewis (1898-1963)

Gratitude transforms how we see the journey. It helps us focus on what we have instead of what we lack. By appreciating each moment, we find joy even in the challenges. This section is about nurturing a grateful heart and seeing the beauty. With gratitude, every step becomes meaningful.

I am grateful for the lessons and growth that come from every experience.

I choose to see the good in each moment, even during challenges.

I appreciate the progress I've made, no matter how small.

I find joy in the journey
and trust it is leading
me where I need to be.

I am thankful for the
strength and resilience
I gain along the way.

I focus on the blessings in my life and let gratitude guide my thoughts.

I celebrate each step
forward, knowing
it brings me closer
to my goals.

I am grateful for the process that shapes me into my best self.

VISUALIZING
SUCCESS

"Be sure you put your feet in the right place, then stand firm."
Abraham Lincoln (1809 – 1865) 16th President of the United States

Success begins with a clear vision. When you can see your goals, you create a path to achieve them. Visualization helps you focus your energy and stay motivated. This section is about imagining your success and believing in your ability to reach it. With a strong vision, goals are achievable and possible.

I see my goals and
trust in my ability
to achieve them.

I focus my thoughts on success and let them guide my actions.

I visualize my future
with confidence
and excitement.

I am creating the life I desire, one step at a time.

I trust my vision to lead
me toward my dreams.

I align my actions
with the success I
see for myself.

I am inspired and motivated by the vision of my future.

I believe in my ability
to turn my dreams
into reality.

IN
CLOSING

"Faithful servants never retire. You can retire from your career, but you will never retire from serving God."
Rick Warren (1954 -)

As you finish this book, may you feel inspired and encouraged. Each section we explored is a step toward trusting the process of life. Starting where you are, embracing change, overcoming obstacles, cultivating patience, building confidence, finding gratitude, and visualizing success all connect to form a path of growth.

The affirmations in this book are not just words. They are tools to help you see things differently and stay strong. Revisit them often. Let them remind you of your strength and guide you when the road feels hard. Each time you read them; you reinforce the positive changes you are making

Trusting the process is not always easy. It takes faith and persistence, but it is always worth it. You have what you need within you to succeed. Believe in yourself, stay focused on your vision, and take each step with courage. Your journey is unique, and every moment matters.

As a contemporary Christian music songwriter and singer Kari Jobe (1981 -) says: "When the Lord opens a door, walk through it. If He doesn't, just trust."

Thank you. I am grateful for your time. May these affirmations continue to uplift and support you as you move forward. Trust the process and keep shining.

With gratitude and belief in your journey, enjoy,

Nancy Moorhouse
February, 2025